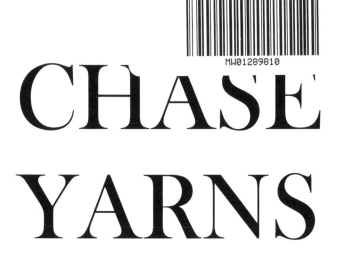

# CHASE YARNS

## an untold story

DANIEL BOROVIK

*For my late chivalrous grandfather, Poppy, whom I daily aspire to be; for my intelligent, inclusive late grandmother Memaw; for my affectionate grandma Marie; for my strong, self-sacrificial parents; for each one of my great-hearted, unique five siblings; for my entirely loving friend Jen; for my undeservingly helpful, caring friends Joe and Rob; for my wise, inspirational mentor Ed; for incredibly respectful DPDR spokesman and writer Jeffrey Abugel; for my talented friend and remarkable filmmaker Jonathan Caouette; and for all sufferers and supporters. – Chase Yarns*

■

*To my mother and father, Yelena and Boris; to my brother Josh; grandparents Zina, Bella, and Michael; to all the friends who supported me through this journey, and to everyone in this world who lives each day with mental illness. – Daniel Borovik*

# Contents

# Introduction

The date was Friday, July 21 of 2017, and I'd just arrived home from the LA Fitness in Beachwood, Ohio. It had been less than a week since I returned to the U.S. from a two-week trip to Israel. So I decided to relax and smoke some marijuana – something I'd done thousands of times the last six years. I couldn't say what happened this time, but it wasn't good.

The panic attack I faced after smoking forever changed my life and how I view it. And it was only after that that I started noticing signs of the disorder which is the focus of this book. I don't blame the marijuana for the disorder – it's hard to blame anything, because it came so randomly – but I am lucky to have a strong support system that helped, and continues to help, me through the difficult times.

That's who I am, Daniel Borovik. I struggle with a psychological disorder called DDD: depersonalization-derealization disorder. This disorder has affected my life greatly, and until I met a young man named Chase Yarns – who suffers from the same condition and whose struggles I truly understand – it was tough to confront alone.

I want the world to know about this disorder, and I want the world to understand the struggles that those with it go through. Chase, I learned, has a unique story. I am thankful that he is willing to speak about it, showing others that they are not alone, and that there are ways to cope, no matter how difficult it may be.

I also hope that this book will inspire more research on DDD so that every clinic, hospital, and doctor knows about it and can properly help treat it. It is only this sort of knowledgeable care, coupled with the backing of a strong support group of those who understand and can empathize, that will help all those who suffer from these effects.

The following story is told and narrated by Chase Yarns. It is a taste of what the difficult reality is like for people with DDD.

---

## Timeline of Events

I developed depersonalization-derealization disorder on an otherwise normal summer day, Aug. 23, 2016. I started smoking marijuana late in the evening, and a short time later, was in the emergency room at the local hospital in Ithaca, New York.

I was in the emergency room until 5 a.m. the next morning. My first class started a few hours later at 8 a.m., and I was determined to go.

But I was still not feeling normal when, on returning from the ER to walk to class with my sister, I couldn't recognize her. She looked vaguely familiar, and yet vaguely unfamiliar – like a stranger one has run into multiple times, but you don't know their name or anything about them.

Things got even worse during my third class of the day. I couldn't handle the feelings I was getting – I broke down in the middle of class, the professor called off the lecture, and then personally escorted me to the college's medical center to get checked out. I was getting worse and worse.

This was just the beginning of my struggles with DDD. For two to three weeks after my first visit to the ER and to the on-campus medical center, I saw a variety of therapists who could not quite place me. Seeing no improvement or betterment of my condition, soon I was hospitalized in Ithaca, New York for five days. When I got out, I spent a month recuperating in that city before going home to Scranton, PA, on medical leave from college.

Soon after, I was admitted to the Scranton psychiatric unit for nine days. Within 24 hours, however, they had extended my stay to 14 days.

After this 14-day stay, I was discharged for a week. Not more than a week later, I was back at the same facility for 42 days. Over the course of this stay, I began to receive 11 electroconvulsive therapy treatments, turning 19-years-old just before the last of these treatments on March 3.

In late March, I returned to the Scranton psychiatric unit for 11 days. Then I was out for another month before attempting suicide on the Freedom Bridge in Clarks Summit, PA. That was May 4, 2017, and after that incident, I was back at the Scranton facilities for 26 days.

My family then sent me to a retreat in Maryland for 20 days. Things were still getting no better, though, and I was admitted to a Baltimore hospital for 36 days immediately after my discharge from the retreat.

On Oct. 5, 2017, I went back to the psychiatric unit in Scranton for 15 days. When I was discharged this last time, the slip containing my discharge information listed my follow-up doctor as "Dr. Phil."

In total, I had spent 158 days in psychiatric hospitals spanning three states, with an additional 20 days at a residential treatment center in Maryland.

During the last visit, Dr. Phil became interested in my case, and brought me onto his show. The recording took place on Oct. 25, 2017 and aired on Dec. 19.

After this, I went to a few conferences on depersonalization disorders in New York City. There I met Jeff Abugel, author of *Stranger to My Self* and co-author of *Feeling Unreal*. I continue to struggle with the disorder today.

---

# Chapter 1: *What is DPDR?*

DPDR is not the same thing as DDD.

DDD is depersonalization-derealization disorder, the actual diagnosis of the condition (it used to be called DPD, or "depersonalization disorder," but that acronym has since been replaced by DDD).

DPDR, however, stands for depersonalization-derealization, which is the acronym for the symptoms that one with DDD has. If you have DDD, you experience DPDR.

It would be easy to write the medical terms and jargon used to describe these symptoms. They are readily available on many informative websites and internet support pages. However, I would rather describe what DPDR *feels* like to me, in the hopes that it will more clearly communicate just what all the medical explanations mean for a living, human individual.

To me, depersonalization is when I am obviously detached from myself, but not necessarily just my personality. This is a different symptom than derealization, which I will describe shortly. It's important to remember, however, that depersonalization is eminently concerned with the self.

Depersonalization is like I am a foreign substance to myself: physically, everything about me is foreign, and I have trouble recognizing my own person. Some people describe it as looking into a mirror and not recognizing the person that stands before you. This is absolutely true; however, it is much more than that. The analogy does not explain the otherworldly feeling one gets from seeing their own body – which, logically, they know to be theirs – as a stranger, as someone you might run into on the sidewalk, and never see again.

But my first symptom of DDD was the dreamlike, artificial perception of the world in derealization, not depersonalization. Derealization is the symptom one gets regarding the world around them, the world that exists outside them – rather than the world within them.

Derealization was the very first thing that I overpoweringly experienced. And it shocked me. It was like I was floating just outside myself – not hallucinating or anything, as many people mistakenly think – but a very clear, very detached third-party viewing of my own body and the world in which it existed. The physical world was foreign to me. Inanimate objects did not make sense; I couldn't recognize them; they were not real; and the floating sensation I experienced was not only the floating of my body, but the floating of my body through this suddenly strange world with all its strange and unreal surroundings.

The thing that got me was the sensation of it all. I felt hyperaware of being alive – a hyperaware consciousness of this strange body's existence and movement, which for my whole life I always had, and continue to, call "mine." It was an overwhelming, indescribable feeling of, "whoa, I'm alive – I'm alive and being alive freaks me out, being alive causes this odd and freaky sensation."

That is the closest feeling I can relate: that you feel like you're floating, and though your five senses work perfectly well, they just don't seem to be your old five senses you used to love and know – although your mind may still be yours and, logically, you know that it is one with your body and your senses. And you think this feeling is going to end, until it doesn't.

Nothing has affected my life so much as DPDR. Not even the good things like the accolades and achievements we get in school, and that propel us on a path to a better future. When I was in high school I was in the National Honor Society, and I made the honor roll every quarter of every year. I was very active and played three sports: indoor track in the winter, outdoor track in the spring, and cross country in the summer and fall. I actually excelled at that – long-distance running was my forte. In this as well as most other subjects in school, I did fairly well.

Out of the four of us siblings in the family (we were quadruplets – much more on this later) I was the first one to get a job and the first one to get my license. I was always kind of the first to do everything in my family, a go-getter. I thought big, was a hard worker and had a good social life. But DPDR does not consider those factors at all.

---

# Chapter 2: *A Day In The Life*

Usually, I can't fall asleep until four o'clock in the morning, and sleep paralysis comes almost every night. Sometimes, it goes away for a couple of weeks, but then it will come back for a day or more. I wish I could say it was only insomnia – but it is that and much more.

If I can manage to get to sleep, I will usually take a shower right after waking up. That shower is a pivotal moment in my day. It's a really big trigger for the depersonalization – because when you're washing yourself, you experience these automatic, overwhelming feelings that weird you out, and make you say, "whoa, this is my body," and, "whoa, this is really freaky and weird." Your mind can't help but separate yourself from the body that you are washing.

When I get out of the shower, I am usually on my way to one of three of my weekly psychologist appointments. On top of that, there is the life coach, whom I see twice a week, and then one of various specialists. Currently I have a Lyme specialist, but I've had an OCD specialist as well. Lots and lots of appointments.

Recently, I've been getting out a little more, which includes volunteering at the Republican office in Scranton. But that job took a little getting used to – I really had to ground myself in the office, and it took a long time to make it familiar. As with most things, it was the hardest in the beginning. But it's still a bit of a pain now because it's a 15-minute drive from my house. And that freaks me out, driving.

My day is unorganized. I try to keep a schedule, but it just won't work. But the thing is, it was never like this before. I worked three summer jobs during high school: a cashier at a grocery store, a dishwasher at a restaurant, and a running coach for 8- to 12-year-olds in the summers. I even had the cashier job throughout all of school and the sports seasons.

Now I can't work. I tried going back to work somewhere around five times, but I get panic attacks. That's so unlike me – I always wanted to work and make money, just like everyone else. I remember my great aunt recently telling me that, "Oh, when you see all of your siblings making the big bucks, then you'll start working." I wanted to tell her, no, that's not how it works.

People think that they know the true Chase Yarns. I still have the same mannerisms, the same way of speaking, the same humor (if I can have it), and the same facial expressions. But they see the tiny amount of something else that I reveal – something that is not the Chase they think they know.

It all changed so fast. I was always working and playing sports and being active and social. It seems funny to me now that my parents would ever say, "Chase, you're doing too much." Which they did.

---

# Chapter 3: *Childhood*

The main thing to know about my childhood is that I was a quadruplet. My mom had four babies at the same time (on top of the two sons she already had from another marriage, who are my half-brothers). To me, that was perfectly normal because that's all I ever knew in life. But as I got older, I realized just how odd it was – having four kids all at once, that would be a lot. I don't know how my mom did it.

We were premature at 31.5 weeks and, unsurprisingly, tiny. I was 2 lbs. 2 oz. The other three were 3.5 lbs. In fact, I was the reason why the pregnancy was so early, as I had stopped growing. But we came out all right, which is surprising given that many quadruplets are born with blindness or other physical ailments.

It was a big thing in the area where I grew up that my mom gave birth to quadruplets. We were the first and only ones in the county, actually. My dad had been a cop, and many people knew him and our family. So we were always kind of in the spotlight already, and when the quadruplets came, even more so. After that, the local broadcast stations and the papers were all coming to my mom for stories. They were there so much we kids even got close to some of them as we grew up. But it was something about the oversized stroller with four babies in a row which my mom would push down the sidewalk – we were the talk of the town at the time.

After our birth, my mother joined a "multiples" group with other people who had triplets or more. The group was called M.O.S.T., or Mother of Super Twins, and when I was around four years old, a message came across the group saying The Tonight Show was looking for super-twin guests for one of its episodes. So we submitted a video, and my mom got a call with an invitation to the show.

It was our fifth birthday when we were on The Tonight Show with Jay Leno. John Travolta was the guest that night, and we got to meet him. Jay Leno himself treated us very nicely, and gave us a free trip to Disneyland for coming on. When we got back home, of course, we were talked about even more for being on the show. I liked the show very much, and I remember most of what it was like. I vividly recall looking out into the audience and seeing all the people focusing their attention on us. They were genuinely curious about what it was like to live in such a family.

I doubt my mother thought of all the extra things she'd have to do to take care of quadruplets. It's definitely something that no one would realize until it's happened and they are forced to do those things. Besides the obvious, "Oh, the pregnancy itself is gonna be bad," there's feeding four mouths every day and night, taking them all to their different activities and practices, cosigning for four separate college tuitions when they grow older, and so much more.

The four of us were in the same class from preschool to fourth grade. We all had the same teacher in every new grade we entered those years, so they would get to know our lives pretty well.

Nothing really changed in grades five and six either. That started in seventh grade, when we began to do our own thing. Then throughout high school, things were completely different. Some courses overlapped, of course, but there were many more options to choose from, and we would sometimes have classes with each other and sometimes not. It was an interesting experience to grow up with that. We knew all the same drama, and it was impossible to escape that. But it was also an advantage to have three friends you could always count on in the same grade, because they were your siblings. We studied and did homework together, and helped each other out.

---

# Chapter 4: *Before DDD*

After high school, three of us went to the same college in upstate New York, while one, my brother, went to a school in central Pennsylvania, which was further away from home than the rest of us were, even though it was in the same state.

I was really excited for college. I was never a small thinker, and I had always been a hard worker. College was where I was going to start turning my big ideas into reality, where I was going to chase my ambition and achieve real things. What I really wanted was a career, a good career, and having a wife and kids who loved me and who I could amply support. For some reason the thought of that excited me more than the regular college kid. My mind was always toward the future. I just wanted to be in the real world.

I was very outgoing when I got to college. This makes sense, as I received the "senior superlative" recognition for being the most talkative person my last year in high school. A lot of people knew I was really goofy, too, kind of the class clown. But I was friends with everyone. It didn't matter who you were – popular, druggy, whoever – I'd have a good time with you if you had a good time with me, and we'd be friends. I just didn't care who you were. I talked to anyone.

I also have a very silly personality. Sometimes I would get kicked out of class for laughing. But at the same time I did really well in academics, and was a very good student. I think people would mostly describe me as being energetic, fun, outgoing, and a hard worker. I always made room for having fun in school, in the sports and activities I did, and when I was hanging out with my friends.

---

# Chapter 5: *Getting DDD*

I believe it was August 23 of 2016, the day before classes began at my college. I wasn't stressed about school, I wasn't stressed about my life – I wasn't stressed about anything in particular, really. And that's when I smoked. So it's pretty obvious to me that the trigger for this disorder of mine was marijuana.

It was my first time smoking. But everyone has a first time doing that, and most people come out just fine, even if it's a bit of a weird or scary experience. Also, I didn't decide to smoke because I felt terrible or needed relief or something. I wasn't even pressured to do it. It was just like, "Hey, why not try smoking pot."

Before this, I had never touched pot. I'd never done any sort of drug, actually. To this day I've never even gone to an underage drinking party. I still drank a handful of times, but that was just with close friends. And I never got really drunk like a lot of people, or even finished a full glass of beer or wine (to this day). I was always able to control myself. I never knew what it was like when people talked about being trashed or blacked out or out of their mind, because I hadn't done that.

On the day of the incident, one of my best friends from high school texted me asking to hangout and smoke. We went to schools in the same town, so we could see each other easily. It was a really short, simple text, totally nonchalant: "Hey, wanna smoke?" I said sure.

So he drove to my college and picked me up. Then we went to this parking lot – I think it was an abandoned lot or something. He brought out the pot but, the thing was, we didn't have a regular bong. He didn't have anything for a joint or a blunt either, so we smoked out of an apple, which I found out was a really popular thing to do. He took an apple, dug a hole in the top, made a smaller hole through the side, and then that's where I took my inhales.

He smoked, and then he handed it to me and I took some pretty heavy inhales. He said, "You gotta get it in your lungs," so he emphasized that I take deep drags on it. And, yeah, I made sure I got it in there. And I kept on going, because I wasn't really feeling it. So we started driving around waiting for it to kick in, and I was thinking to myself that I didn't really feel any different.

I experienced my first symptom of derealization shortly after. It was the first moment, the start of everything. We had parked in the downtown Ithaca Commons and I stepped out of the car. I vividly remember walking out to the sidewalk, looking around, and feeling like I was in a totally different dimension.

I wouldn't say that anything looked different, because it didn't really. But everything felt different. I felt floaty. My five senses were all off. The overpowering sensation was that I was totally, completely removed from reality. I didn't believe I was out of reality – because I could still logically think – but I couldn't stop *feeling* that I was. And I just kept getting more and more detached from my body, my soul, my surroundings. It was very uncomfortable.

I tried to tell my friend how I was feeling. I turned to him and said, "Whoa, I feel really weird. This isn't good." And of course, he was laughing. He was just thinking that his friend was having a really bad high or something. So that's when we started walking to try to get the feeling away. But it just kept hitting me, hitting me and hitting me. Then my heart started to flutter, and that's when things got really, really bad.

As a long-distance runner, I knew what it was like to have a very rapid heart rate. But what I experienced then was not a rapid heart rate. It felt exactly like what you would think a heart attack would feel like. Super-aggressive physical flutters, inconstant and irregular. I really did think I was having a heart attack.

I could literally feel my heart pounding very, very rapidly, and I thought I was dying. I thought my brain was preparing its body for death, even though I wasn't in any physical danger.

That extreme feeling of being close to death lasted about 10 seconds, and I could have sworn that I was gone. When I just barely came back around to things, we were still walking, and I was totally out of it. I kept having to put my hand on my chest, because my heart would not stop fluttering violently. I would stop walking, be forced to check my heart, keep walking, then stop and have to check my heart again. I know just putting my hand to my heart would not have done anything to calm it, but it would just not stop fluttering.

Then we went into a convenience store and I bought one of those Naked brand smoothies. I took a few sips from it, but it couldn't calm me down. I was still telling my friend, "This is not good. Something's way off. My heart is fluttering" – and he didn't understand that at all. I just remember him laughing a lot, still thinking I was only really high.

But then I could see him get a little worried, and he said, "Oh, I'm going to take you back to your dorm." So he drove me back to the dorm, and I said something like, "Can you stay with me?" Because I didn't want to be alone if something was going to happen to me, you know. And he said, "Well, I kind of have to go right now." But I think he was just nervous that he was going to get in trouble – that's how bad it was.

I remember when I was in the Ithaca Commons first getting the feeling, I saw another friend who I graduated with, but he was going to Cornell. He was further down on the sidewalk. I was like, "Oh my gosh, does he realize that I'm way out of it or high or anything like that?"

But then he came up and we started talking. Yet things were off – he looked unfamiliar. Everyone looked unfamiliar. I saw both him and another friend on the sidewalk and they were just so unfamiliar. I didn't have paranoia, but when I was walking, I was hyperaware of everything.

Ithaca has brick roads. When I was walking along one of these, I was kind of questioning if there was pavement. But it was a whole brick road, and when I realized that, it completely threw me off guard.

There were also benches, and a metal sculpture of a woman sitting on one of the benches. And when I was walking around feeling completely out of it, I was questioning to myself, "Is that girl sitting on that bench actually a real girl, but I'm seeing her as a figure?" I had a lot of these kinds of feelings, and they were tripping me out. I wasn't tripping like people do on harder drugs, of course, but I was definitely tripping out, and at one point I questioned whether I was hallucinating. In the end, though, I wasn't.

A little while later, after my friend had dropped me off at my dorm, he asked, "Are you gonna be okay?" I was uncertain when I responded. I said, "Yeah, I guess," knowing full well that I actually was not going to be okay.

When I got inside my dorm, I started talking to my roommate. It's embarrassing to think back on – it would have been embarrassing at the time if I wasn't in crisis mode. I was asking him about things because he had smoked pot. I said, "Have you ever felt this way before?" And he said no.

I started to freak out. This wasn't good. It felt like I was having a heart attack still and I was feeling floaty and my vision was off – I couldn't tell you why or how my vision was off, but it was. Tears formed up in my eyes, I was so scared and confused at what was happening to me. I started crying, maybe even sobbing, and I went to our floor's resident assistant, and they called an ambulance. I smoked around 9 p.m., and I was taken off in the ambulance not long after at all, probably around 10 p.m.

I was on my way to the hospital in the ambulance. It might have been campus security taking me to Ithaca's hospital – it's very hard to remember, when I was feeling the way I was. And when I got to the emergency room, I was crying. Something's wrong with my heart or my vision, I remember saying. These moments arriving at the ER are so vivid to me still. Something was off – something major. But I couldn't figure out how to describe it. Whatever it was, it wasn't little. It was something beyond words.

I never had exaggerated my pains before. So I was trying to tell the doctor, "This is huge, this is really, really bad." But he wasn't really understanding what I was saying. He didn't even admit to describe it as a panic attack. He didn't say anything about it; just, "You're physically fine. Go home."

The doctor told me to go home around 5 a.m. So I did. I paid cash for a cab back to my dorm, because if I paid with my debit card, my parents would have seen it. I arrived back at my dorm at about 5:30 a.m. Then, I had to wake up for my first class at 8 a.m. So I got only about an hour of sleep once back in my dorm, after spending all night awake in the hospital.

I saw my sister, and we were going to walk to our first class together. Only something was extremely, horribly different about her – not about her, per se, but about how I saw her. I looked at her face and did not recognize her at all. I felt like I was kind of behind a screen, and very floaty. But I wanted to tell her what had happened to me, and try to explain how I was feeling. So I just told her, "oh my gosh, I have to tell you a story." Because she would have known something was up.

I went to my first class completely zoned-out. Then I went to my second class, also completely zoned-out, and still feeling depersonalized and derealized, even though at the time I didn't know what those words were at all.

My third class was a seminar. There were six people in it. But at this point in the day, I was only feeling worse and worse. So I went up to my professor and said, "I'm not feeling good. I smoked marijuana last night. I still feel out of it and panicky." She could really tell that it was as bad as it was, because she canceled the class and personally walked me to the medical center on campus.

The nurse at the medical center told me that I should tell my parents what's going on. This was a really tough thing for me to do, and not just because I didn't know how to explain what was happening to me. I was going to school for physical therapy, and I had actually already got accepted into Ithaca College's doctorate physical therapy program. I'd be ashamed to let me parents know what I had done, and then to tell them that whatever it did to me was so serious and scary. But I called anyway.

My mom was angry and surprised when I told her I smoked pot. She asked the question rhetorically back to me, as if she didn't believe that I'd do that kind of thing. But I was just trying to get the message across to her: "No, this is a big deal. Something's wrong with me health-wise." And eventually, after we kept talking about it, she realized that it was serious, and that we might have to do something.

After those eventful first couple of days, I just tried to get on with things as normal and go to all my classes and stuff. During those few following weeks, I remember getting into the habit of calling my best friend from high school up, who went to school in Philadelphia. I would call him in the middle of the night, at midnight, and ask him very deep, philosophical, existential questions, like "What is life?" or "What does a mother mean?" Of course I knew what a mother meant biologically, but I would ask things like what does that kind of relationship actually mean, and what does it mean to be a son? To be a mother? That was weeks after all this happened, and I was still at school. My friend kind of laughed at all that.

I would also call him and try to explain how I was feeling, saying things like, "I feel really weird, and I can't really explain why." And a lot of other people who knew me – they would have said this habit of calling my friend was different for me, because I've never annoyed people that much. So I guess people kind of knew something was up, but they definitely didn't know or understand the depth of the problem. Still to this day two years later, they don't get the depths no matter how much I talk about it or try to explain it.

I had started seeing a counselor twice a week there on campus. Ithaca's a pretty global town, and the people are on the whole pretty smart and worldly. So in my appointments I always heard talk about enlightenment and stuff like that. I just kept feeling weird, though.

I have an extremely vivid memory of the first time I walked into the counseling center. There was a black woman who was the secretary. She was an older woman, about middle-aged. I remember so clearly going there, walking up to her and just bawling my eyes out. I had to fill this form out every time and I just couldn't focus.

This form caused so many problems for me. It was on a laptop and I just couldn't do it. I was crying, asking someone, anyone, to please help me, I was totally out of it. And I just assumed the secretary could see it.

But if I actually try to think about that day, thinking on it back from this far in the future, I probably looked normal – just like I was crying because I'd had a bad day or a rough week. But that is the furthest from what I was feeling internally. Inside the locked box of my mind and my feelings, I was experiencing something I've never experienced before. Something that's out of this world, in the most literal sense.

I remember sobbing to the secretary, "I feel terrible, I need more than just a counselor." And she's like, "Just try to fill out the form, we need that information." I just told her that I couldn't. I couldn't focus. I felt really trippy, like I couldn't do anything, not even the most menial tasks. Actually, it felt like I was going to faint at that moment. But I didn't actually faint, and she helped

me with the system and eventually got me to the
therapist.

A couple weeks after that I was hospitalized for the first
time in Ithaca. I was in a psychiatric unit, so that was
interesting. And it was my first time in that sort of a unit
as well. My parents drove from Scranton, PA to Ithaca,
NY to see me and try to get things worked out.

---

# Chapter 6: *First Hospital Visits*

Back to my first visit to the college's medical center, where the nurse I talked to had me call my mom in front of her. After that was over, the nurse told me, "It's probably only gonna last twenty four to forty eight hours, at most." But it never went away. I tried to keep going to classes, but obviously I couldn't focus at all. I'd sob all the time. I'd text and call people in the middle of the night. And that was definitely unlike me.

As described in the previous chapter, after some weeks I was admitted for the first time to the psychiatric unit of a hospital in Ithaca. At the time I thought, "Wow, they're just going to put me on some medications and fix me right up. It will be real simple and real quick, just like that." But it wasn't.

It was for just under a week this first time. My doctor's name was Dr. Garcia, and he kind of laughed at all the things I was saying to him. He acted a bit like it wasn't serious at all. I forget a lot of what happened there, because I was still under the overwhelming symptoms of the onset of this disorder. I don't even remember too much about that therapy – I don't remember the therapist or much about that place at all. But I do remember this one kid I met. He had gone to Cornell and was a really good artist, and was bipolar.

When I first walked into the hospital room with my parents, they were holding my hand. I sat on the bed and began crying, and so did they – it was their goodbye to me for the week. But I felt reassured with all the medical staff's encouragement of, "Oh, we're going to get you better, you'll be good." My parents believed that too. It was a really weird time.

I started getting suicidal thoughts almost immediately after arriving there. It wasn't because I thought I was helpless. It was because I just couldn't take the pain. And the thoughts only got stronger and stronger as the months and years went by.

After five days, I got out of the hospital and was going to try to return to classes and everything normal. But I was still out of it. So I realized that I'd have to go home on medical leave, and suspend the progression of my degree, which was a big disappointment.

I went on medical leave, sure, but now I've been out of there for so long that it's not medical leave anymore. I had to drop out, basically. And that fact is a little bit jarring – it's totally unlike me, because I was always such a good student. I was in National Honor Society, made the honor roll every quarter, got straight A's, took AP classes, and was involved in athletics.

Lots of what happened in that time period is a blur. I have all the records of my hospital visits and everything, but they are sharper than my own memory. Lots of what my memory consists of is just the feelings, thoughts and confusion of that time. The next hospital I was admitted to was back home in Scranton. That was just over a month after I got out of the psychiatric unit in Ithaca, and then went back home on medical leave.

When I got to that second hospital, I was very, very suicidal, and still just as out of it as before – perhaps more so. And that just kept going on and on, for a total of 158 days in the various hospitals spread over eight separate admittances. And that was all within just around a year of getting DDD, when I was just 18 years old. For three of those hospitalizations, in fact, I was "302'd," which means I had to be in the hospital involuntarily, because I couldn't be left on my own.

It's very weird being in a psychiatric ward. You meet all these really fascinating people when you're there for so long. I was in there a lot longer than other people too, sometimes. Some people didn't realize just how long it had been. But I was making friends with all kinds of people – schizophrenics, people with psychosis, sociopaths, psychopaths, and more.

It wasn't scary being there with all of them. Maybe it would have been slightly un-normal if everything else in my life weren't so un-normal at the time. Sure, it was weird meeting all these different kinds of people, but I became friends with them. I became friends with people who were severely, severely depressed, and people who had really bad panic disorders or people who'd had bad overdoses. Yes, a lot of the people in there had had overdoses.

I remember seeing a guy who'd been 302'd because he slit his own throat. He had staples in his throat now where the doctors had fixed him up. The story was that he was trying to hang himself in his basement when his girlfriend came downstairs and caught him. But he had a knife, and his will to kill himself was so strong that he put it up to his own throat and sliced it. So I saw the staples there on his throat. I was friends with him.

I was also friends with a woman who had shot herself in the head and survived. She had staples all over her head, and was somewhere around 40 years old. She was receiving ECT (eletrocompulsive therapy) treatments with me as well.

Speaking of ECT treatments, I underwent a total of 11 of them. The last one occurred when I was 19 years old. The others were when I was still just 18. Usually, you don't get those kinds of treatments until you are 40 or so. Your brain doesn't even fully develop until you're 27, so obviously I was a bit young at the time.

The ECT treatments were never really at my own request – they were part of the medical staff's suggestions for treatment, obviously. You never go into a hospital and say, "Hey, let's get some ECTs." But I had been in the hospital so much that I was really doing anything at this point. Going to the surgery room and putting me under for the ECTs became commonplace.

Throughout my hospital visits, I was in pain, depressed, anxious, depersonalized and derealized. But my doctor didn't really recognize the disorder. In fact, I only found out about the term "depersonalization" after many weeks in the whole situation, and then I started using that and similar terms. But when I got hospitalized, my doctor thought it must be psychosis or schizophrenia or something. I don't really think he believed in the disorder I have, because a lot of people actually don't. But they should, because many people, myself included, actually suffer greatly from it, and it's also in the DSM, or Diagnostic and Statistical Manual of Mental Disorders. It's known as one of the dissociative disorders.

That was the doctor that gave me 11 ECTs at 18 and 19 years old. They would just put me under anesthesia, hook in the IV, and that was it. The first treatment was the first time I was ever on anesthesia as well.

Going under anesthesia didn't make me more anxious. I only felt a little bit that way when they would put the mask on and say, "You're going out." But at that point in this whole series of events, I was so numb to everything. It didn't matter to me anymore. I was already suffering terribly – nothing else scared me. It's kind of funny how these sorts of things, getting the ECT treatments and all that, would probably be pretty traumatizing to a normal person; but because I had this condition so severely, and was suffering so much under its effects, it was different for me. Anything that gave me the hope of getting rid of it I was willing to try. And even to this day, I've still got it chronically. I have one of the more severe cases, obviously.

But a lot of the stuff I was seeing, the disgusting and the terrible stuff, really didn't faze me. My heart rate might have gone up a bit right before they put on the oxygen mask and knocked me out. But each time I'd wake up, and then would come the commonplace question that a nurse would ask me to gauge how aware I was – something like, "Who's the president?" And each time I'd give the right answer, Donald Trump.

Speaking of Trump, I was one of his supporters, though I was hospitalized at the time of his inauguration. It was hard to care about and put a lot of effort into following the election when I was always in a psychiatric unit. I was even hospitalized for Christmas – it was endless.

To this day I'm still interested in and involved with politics. But you know, there are so many things that I logically care about, but at the end of the day, my mental health and how I'm doing come first. In the end, I don't care about politics – maybe I don't even care about relationships with friends so much. What matters to me is my mental health and my health in general. I don't think people understand that mental health is all we have.

You can be in any physical circumstance, you can have the worst situation, you can even be disabled – but if you have decent or good mental health, that's all that matters. Because it is through the lens of your mind that you see and understand and appreciate the world. And when that portion of yourself is somehow off, as happens when you develop DDD, you realize that anything would be better than that.

There are obviously negative things that come with being disabled, or having other physical ailments. And the reason why it can get so bad is because some part of a person's physical makeup is missing or off, and then that affects the mental side of things. Some people are born blind, and some people are born with these weird and fascinating disorders. A lot of times, when they're born with it, they say, "I wouldn't want anything else." Like someone born without an arm – they might say that's just how things are, and they are okay with it. But if someone is born with both arms, and then loses one at the age of 30, that could really affect not only the physical side of life, but the mental side. And the mental side is where it gets bad. But it all depends on the situation. I continue to always tell people it's all about mental health.

Before all this happened to me, I was ignorant of mental health. I thought depressed people were not grateful – I thought suicide was stupid, and would always question why someone would be so selfish to do that, would inflict that sort of pain and emotional trauma on their families. Now I have totally different opinions on that, and a lot of other things. I used to think depressed people would exaggerate, and I used to think they were lazy. But what I didn't realize was how debilitating it all was. How truly, truly debilitating. And I learned that the hard way; it had to happen to me.

---

# Chapter 7: *Hospitals and Medications*

I'd like to write a little bit more about the hospital. At one time I was threatened to go to a state hospital long-term. It was so frustrating because no one knew what I was talking about. They just couldn't understand what I was attempting to describe to them. And because they couldn't understand that, I don't think they understood just how serious it was either.

I was in the padded room three times at the Geisinger Community Medical Center in Scranton, PA. Two of those times, I told the people, "Just knock me out. I am in so much pain, just knock me out. I don't want to hurt anyone, so just knock me out." So they knocked me out.

The third time I was in the padded room, it was the rubber room. Blue-padded, all mats. And that's where they put the crazies. I was in that room. And I was in so much pain, so they just knocked me out again. They injected me in the butt.

But one of the times I was in the padded room was because I was on Haldol and I had tardive dyskinesia, which is a condition affecting the nervous system usually caused by the long-term use of psychiatric drugs. Most often, the symptoms include involuntary movements, such as the rapid blinking of eyes or movements of the mouth. It is a terrible, terrible condition.

I've been on every medication. I was on anti-psychotics, anti-depressants, benzos – anything you can think of. A lot of medications.

I think schizophrenics take Haldol. I was on mood stabilizers as well. But the time I was on Haldol was when I got tardive dyskinesia. It manifested itself in me as involuntary upward movements of my arm. The other was effectively crippled. My tongue also started to hang out, and I think I even stopped breathing once. That was really scary. But then again, nothing really shocked me too much; at that point I was just numb to everything.

When the problems with my arms started, I went off to a mental health worker and said, "Look, my arm's crippled and everything." But I had already found out in weekly medicine information sessions that such behavior was a common side effect of Haldol. But I still went to a mental health worker and asked, "Can someone help me? Because my arm is doing weird stuff." And she said back to me, "Oh, do you need Ativan?" (Ativan is a benzodiazepine, which is supposed to calm you down, almost like alcohol does.) And I said, "Ativan? I don't need Ativan," and was thinking to myself, "Are you stupid?" So I had to yell to get a nurse instead. Mental health workers are not nurses, so it doesn't take as much to become one.

But there was another medication to reverse the effect, and that's why I was in the padded room. They had to inject me in the butt with Cogentin, which is supposed to get rid of the tardive dyskinesia. I passed out when they gave me that.

It was really weird just hanging around people in the psychiatric unit all day. The chairs were also extremely uncomfortable, but you couldn't sleep in your room too much or else they'd lock your doors – if you spent too much time in your room alone.

What really killed me was that I couldn't go outside the hospital. You weren't allowed to leave, and, naturally, it was very confining and restricting. Obviously you don't have your phone on you either. But it wasn't really the phone I was bummed out about. It was the internet. "Can I go on Youtube? Can I go on Google and search this?" As for my dress, a lot of the time I was in scrubs.

---

## Chapter 8: *Suicide*

My first actual suicide attempt occurred on May 4 of 2017. This led to two or three involuntary hospitalizations. This was after I had gotten out of multiple extended stays at psychiatric units. Thinking back on that day, I remember leaving my house with a smile on my face. I was kind of happy, because, hey, all the pain was going to end. The pain was going to go away. And I smiled about that.

When I left my house that day, I told my mom I was going to Subway to get some food. Where I really planned to go was the Freedom Bridge, a half-century-old viaduct over South Abington Township named informally after the high rate of suicides that occur there. The bridge is around 170 feet tall.

So I left the house, drove to the bridge, and parked my car in the parking lot of a nearby dentist's office. Around this time the bridge had actually been remodeled to make it more difficult to jump off the side. Something like a six-foot-tall barrier had been installed for that purpose, because it was such a popular place to jump off.

The reason why I chose to jump off the bridge that day was not necessarily because it was popular, but because I knew it would work. I had been hospitalized many times and was living with my parents. I knew there was a high rate of overdoses not working – if I were to do that, someone would find me, pump my stomach full of chemicals, and before I knew it I'd wake up in a hospital in bad physical condition. So I knew that overdosing wasn't really realistic.

I remember the time I looked up a bunch of information about suicide. I would look up graphs and charts and explanations and specific cases. And then, of course, when you're on Google and looking all that stuff up, the suicide line eventually pops up and you say to yourself, "No, I don't want to talk to them. I want to die."

I found a lot of graphs and charts that explained the common forms of taking one's own life. They plotted the duration of it, the time it would take, the intensity from 1 to 10, and more. And the results are actually surprising – falling from a bridge was supposedly not as bad as people thought. So obviously I researched and looked a lot into that, because I wanted the thing to work. I did not want to come back – did not want there to be any chance of me coming back.

I found that people are sometimes funny when they talk about it, because they don't really realize how it sounds. I use this story a lot: my great aunt – different than the one mentioned in Chapter 2 – posted something on Facebook saying, "Suicide doesn't take away the pain, it only puts it onto the family." I disagree with that, because it's not the same pain. It's grieving. The pain of grief is incomparable to the pain of having depersonalization, anxiety and depression. Especially with the first condition, depersonalization, most people in the world don't know what that's like, and they couldn't even imagine it if they wanted to.

Grieving is part of life. Humans are designed to grieve; grief is the catharsis that we involuntarily use to move past any sort of traumatic experience. Yes, suicide is terrible and incredibly painful for other people – I am not denying that, or trying to diminish the impact that those who have lost a loved one to suicide might feel. But I think it's also important to make the point that grief is a different sort of pain from the pain that is experienced by the person suffering, so I felt that that Facebook post was a little stupid in general.

But of course it's a popular post. One of my great aunt's friends commented, "Oh, I wish they would think first before they did such a stupid act." And I felt forced to comment back, "Actually, they think a lot before they do that kind of thing." No one just wakes up and says, "Oh, I'm gonna kill myself" out of the blue. There is always a lot of thought that goes into it, sometimes even a lot of preparation; and it would be naïve to assume that, even if it wasn't "planned for," per se, the thought would not have been germinating for quite a long time inside a person's head.

It is impossible in this world to be unaware of how other people might react to your actions. The problem with those who follow through with suicide is that this consideration of others was just not enough to stop them in the first place. So we shouldn't say that they were selfish and careless. We should feel sorry that the good things in this world, the empathy of other people, was not enough to stop them from doing it.

People today will still ask me, "Hey, Chase, are you glad you're still alive?" And, no matter what I say, I'm still thinking, "No. I wanted to die that day. It wasn't a stupid in-the-moment decision. It was very thought-out. It was a desire of mine."

But I never, ever blame others for saying things like that to me. Because if this was not me – if the roles were reversed – I'd probably be saying the exact same things to them. Because before all this happened, I was the one who thought that depression wasn't real, and that people who committed suicide were selfish and dumb. I thought they couldn't realize how awesome life is, or were incapable of appreciating or being grateful for it.

On the day that I was determined to commit suicide, I parked my car in the dentist's office lot, climbed up a small hill to get to the turnpike and over to the bridge, climbed up the blue bars that acted as a barrier to jumpers like me, and hopped over onto the opposite side of the fence. There was no ledge there, so I was literally hanging by my fingertips and by my feet. My fingers gripped and clung to the narrow blue metal rods separating me from the earth below.

I guess I was there longer than I thought I was. I was there for a while. Eventually, a negotiator came. And I knew this cop's brother. But I think he kind of knew that there was nothing he could tell me that would get me off the fence. I forget the exact specifics of what we talked about, but I remember that feeling passing between us.

There was nothing he could do; I was focused on dying. I didn't care to hear what this cop had to say.

I had actually thrown my shoes over the bridge to count the seconds that it would take to hit the earth below. Four seconds. That was the duration that I would have to go through. Four seconds. My adrenaline is going to surge. Four seconds. For an instant, there's going to be incredible pain. Four seconds. But then it's going to be done. Four seconds.

I was also thinking about the logistics of my fall. Should I turn my neck this way or that? Do I want to land on my feet or on my head? Would I even be able to control my body once it's in the air? At that rate of falling, would any of those questions even matter?

So I put a lot of thought into it. I was thinking about my death more than I was thinking about who was there, or who had gathered around, or who was trying to get me to climb back over the fence to safety. So I don't really remember a lot of that, because I didn't really care about what they had to say.

I was there on the fence a long time. Before I knew it, they had cut a hole through the wired gate, and they got me out from the other side because they could tell that I had no plan to climb back over. And there was no ledge there. I was hanging – at any moment it could have happened. So they had to judge my situation and act quickly, and they determined that that was the best thing to do.

I remember generalities – vagaries – shouting and yelling, "Don't do it! Don't do it!" Blah blah blah. It was like background noise. I'm not listening – it just exists. I was concentrated on one thought, "Let's end this." I was almost at peace, even. My mind had been made up. Things would be better this way. There was still some anxiety, but there was even more peace. I just had to leap.

And when they got me, I was 302'd. Involuntary hospitalization.

I come from a bit of a small town. People come up to me and they act like they know me. They're really friendly. And then I'll go back and ask my dad, "Why is this one person really friendly? Who are they?" And I'll get some answers, because lots of people know each other.

I remember one lady in my community who works at a store I go to. One day after the incident, I walk in and she says to me, "Hey Chase, how are you?" And she gave me a hug. And in my head, I was thinking, "Who the hell is she? She's really nice and all, but why is she hugging me?"

I knew my dad knew this woman, so I went home and asked my dad about her. I said, Dad, there's this woman, and she's really nice and hugs me all the time. She acts like she knows me, but I don't really know who she is.

And my dad says, "Oh, she was there on May fourth." I say, "I didn't know that. I don't remember her."

I think a lot of that is kind of blocked out of my system, because I don't think I was really thinking about anyone there at the time. I don't even remember the ambulance ride to the hospital. Did I even go into an ambulance that day? All I know is that the incident was in the paper, and about 10 people got an award from the Pennsylvania Turnpike Commission for their work to get me down. They gave them all awards and plaques, but I got nothing. That's crazy. I don't know.

But at that time, I needed nothing. Besides relief from this invisible hell.

---

## Chapter 9: *The Retreat*

I was hospitalized that summer in June. It was my seventh hospitalization – after the incident at the bridge, but before the appearance on Dr. Phil.

God bless him; after I got out of the hospital, my dad spent his retirement money to send me to a retreat in Maryland called Sheppard Pratt Retreat, which was tens of thousands of dollars.

Three weeks was the minimum at this place, which is a very famous spot for many forms of psychiatric and psychological recovery. You could have lobster tail every single night for dinner if you wanted to. That's what kind of place this was. And so I did. I had the lobster tail and crab cakes all the time, because I have an expensive taste.

I was there for the minimum amount of time one could stay, which was three weeks or close to it. At the end of my stay there, the doctor, Dr. Carlson, said to me, "Oh, Chase, you kind of sound depressed. You should probably go to the hospital section." And I thought about it and said, "You know what? Why not?" I wasn't actually suicidal at this time, but just thinking about the context, this was the seventh time I was going to be hospitalized.

At the retreat I'd had my own room and all that, with my own TV. The prospect of leaving this and going to a new hospital, however, was nothing to me – I'd been in many hospitals before. But the new hospital was not as nice as the one back home in Scranton, even. Whereas the retreat itself was like a hospital, but much more luxurious.

But my family's not made of money, so that money was coming out of my dad's retirement. We're currently facing a lot of financial problems because of that. And obviously my dad can't retire right now anymore, so that's difficult.

The retreat was a very holistic place. They talked a lot about Eastern medications, Chinese medicine, and things along those lines. They also talked a lot about dialectical behavior therapy, or DBT, which is mix of cognitive and behavioral therapies; and CBT, which is cognitive behavioral therapy. And then, of course, they talked about mindfulness too. But I hate mindfulness. I think it's the stupidest thing in the world for someone with DDD who experiences strong depersonalization and derealization.

Here is why I think mindfulness is the worst thing for DPDR. I admit that it might be good for someone who is clinically depressed or has a panic disorder and anxiety, because mindfulness is all about being in the moment and being aware of your surroundings. And people with depression are usually caught up thinking about the past, while people with anxiety are usually stressing about the future; being in the moment and forgetting those things for a while might help them.

The overall theory of mindfulness is to be in the moment and just look around you and feel the surroundings, appreciate them without holding any judgment for or against them. Your surroundings just exist and you accept them as they are. If you are sitting down, you just feel the chair below you. If you are outside or near a window, you really hear the birds chirping; you don't think, you just listen. And you try to simply hear and feel all those things. And that freaks me out.

Mindfulness is actually a big trigger for depersonalization because the "moment" is exactly the thing that I don't like. I do not want to be in the moment, and that is what mindfulness aims to make you do. A lot of people don't understand that. That's also why I think a lot of people with depersonalization disorder can't relate to a lot of other people, even those with clinical depression or regular anxiety (which some people might mistakenly lump into the same group as DDD). Yes, we may have some of the same symptoms. I've experienced both depression and anxiety. But I know that people with depression and anxiety have not experienced the otherworldly feelings of DPDR.

People don't understand just how painful the "moment" itself is for me, because I'm already very hyperaware of everything, very hyperconscious. Mindfulness tells me to be even *more* hyperaware of things, and even *more* hyperconscious. So it isn't difficult to see that that would freak me out. Even professionals don't really understand that. I don't blame them. It's a tough concept to understand.

And then there's another form of therapy called radical acceptance therapy. That was something else that the people at the retreat focused on and tried to promote.

I was at the retreat for three weeks, and was at the hospital at the retreat for an extra five weeks. In total, I was at Sheppard Pratt for about two months, which included the Fourth of July.

And that was basically my whole summer. And it was really hard because I wasn't suicidal – I went voluntarily. And that meant that I could leave voluntarily as well, with something called a 72-hour notice. If you voluntarily submit yourself to a psychiatric hospital, you can submit this form. It is to request your leaving; and once you submit it, you have 72 hours to leave.

For the most part, if you're clearly not suicidal and have some recognizable coping skills, they will let you go. And that's what I tried to do. I filled out the form, turned it in, called my mom back home in Scranton, and said, "Mom, I just turned in my seventy two hour notice. I'm coming home."

And quite surprisingly, she said, "No. Then I'm not picking you up." I asked her why she wasn't going to pick me up. I wasn't suicidal. The doctor there thought that he knew what was going on, but I don't really think he had a clue. He wasn't even mentioning depersonalization disorder. To all the things that he *was* mentioning, I could only think, "been there, done that."

He didn't know much about anything I was going through.

I thought that, because the retreat had been so nice, the hospital was going to be the same way as well. But I realized that the one I had stayed in back home in Scranton was 10 times better than this one in Maryland. I think it's because the staff at the Maryland hospital were fighting for a pay raise, and a lot of them had left because of it. So they lost a lot of their workers years back, and the other ones were kind of generic, cycling through the hospital.

It was also less than half the size of the Scranton hospital, and some of the workers were downright terrible. There were only two hallways. In the hospital in Scranton, there had been an art room, a lounge, and two TV rooms. At this place in Maryland, there was no art room; and although there was a TV room, you couldn't go in there all the time. That was probably the worst hospitalization I had, by far.

It was also frustrating because I wasn't actually suicidal. I know when I'm actually suicidal, and that knowledge has been a very difficult thing throughout all this. Because I've had a history with suicide or suicidal thoughts and attempts, people can get so worried. The problem is that sometimes, this sort of reputation can get you falsely 302'd, or involuntarily hospitalized. People think you should be in the hospital because you are suicidal, but you know that you're not. So what do you do?

I'm fully aware of when I'm actually planning suicide as opposed to just having the thoughts. Because I've had suicidal thoughts literally every single day since Aug. 23, 2016, when this whole thing began. Not a day has gone by where I haven't thought about it. So there's a difference between that and when I'm planning for it.

But overall, the hospital was not very good. The thing that really got me was the size, and how small it was compared to the one in Scranton.

The size didn't stop me from meeting people who were there at the same time, just like at the other places. For example, there was this 600-pound girl from Dubai who was very friendly. But there were much fewer people who I actually had the chance to interact with, because I was in the young adult unit for people ages 35 and below. So there were probably just 15 of us younger adults. Just thinking back on it, that was a creepy time.

I felt very trapped there in that hospital in Maryland. It was probably about a 3.5-hour drive from home. To me, that's a decent distance. But I don't even remember driving all the way to Maryland for my stay at the retreat. It was all a blur.

---

# Chapter 10: *Suicidal Implications*

It's extremely frustrating to be 302'd, or involuntarily hospitalized, when you aren't actually suicidal.

One time I had a psychologist say, "Chase, you have to go to the hospital because you sound suicidal." And all I could say back was that I wasn't suicidal. So he sent me to the hospital anyway, because he thought I was. And I was there in the hospital for more than eight hours on this occasion. When the doctor came in, I had to explain that I had absolutely no plan. And then, when the delegate came in at the end, she said, "I don't know why your psychologist sent you here." (I've been through several therapists.)

I was in scrubs again in this incident, so I really thought I was going to be put into a psychiatric unit again. But then I went home – because I wasn't suicidal. So that was the one time my psychologist, who has a doctorate, was wrong. He lost my trust after that, and I left him because of it.

The second time I was told to go to the hospital because I was suicidal – when I actually wasn't suicidal – was with my psychiatrist. And this is what leads to the Dr. Phil show eventually. Keep in mind that this is all after the experience at the Maryland retreat and hospital.

After Maryland I went home, and I tried and tried to do things normally, but I was still struggling so much. I was thinking about suicide again, but not actually planning it or anything. So I go to a normal psychiatrist appointment; these kinds of things had become routine to me by then. This time, I'd been kicked out of my house and was staying with a friend. So I was just crying in front of my psychiatrist.

This psychiatrist worked at the hospital I stayed at longer than any other; so far, I had been hospitalized there five times, for a total of 102 days out of 158 (this would be the sixth time I'd go there, and would bump the total up to 117 days in that hospital). And the psychiatrist said to me, "You have to go to the hospital." I said, "Why? I'm not suicidal." And he said back to me, "I'm worried about your safety." I told him, "I'm not."

He was sitting behind his desk when he told me this. My dad was in the room as well; even though I'd been thrown out of the house, he met me and drove me to the appointment, because I didn't have a car. So we're all in this room together while I'm talking to the psychiatrist. I was doing bad at the time, but I didn't bring up anything about suicide. I genuinely remember that I was not suicidal. But still, he said, "You have to go to the hospital."

What the heck. It's actually very traumatizing and scary to think that, since you have a history with it, people can just throw you into the hospital whenever they want to. You attempted suicide one time, but this doesn't mean that you must absolutely be put back in the hospital when you're not even a threat. And this was the second time such a thing had happened to me. People really don't realize how scary that scenario is, especially when you've already been hospitalized seven times. But either way, I had to go. This was the last time I was hospitalized. I went to the psychiatrist appointment without even thinking about that sort of possibility. I didn't know I would have to be hospitalized after.

So he's sitting behind a desk telling me, "Go to a hospital." And I'm like, "No, I'm not suicidal." But I knew he was a doctor at the hospital, so I knew he had the power to put me in even if I didn't want to go, and really didn't need to.

This incident was in early October of 2017. And this is the big thing I came to be known for when I appeared on Dr. Phil, when they falsely used a headline implicating, "Oh, a kid choked his psychiatrist." I totally didn't choke him. That was a different story altogether.

---

# Chapter 11: *The Real Story*

This is the real story of what happened there. I was at my psychiatrist appointment and I was crying. I had been thrown out of the house, and I was going through a rough time. And the only time you should be 302'd is if you're a danger to yourself or to others – a direct threat to someone else or yourself.

This means that you're either suicidal or homicidal or physically harmful with someone. And I wasn't either one of those things, so that was very frustrating.

So when he said that – that I had to go back to the hospital again – I stood from my chair and went to walk out the door. So he runs around his desk and comes up to me, and then we had a confrontation. He said, "You have no choice." And that really sunk in. *You don't have a choice. You're going to be in the hospital again, for the eighth time.*

*You don't have a choice.*

He was going to try to forcefully detain me, and I was going to try to run out. So what I did was I put my hands around his neck. But it wasn't longer than a couple of seconds, and he did not stop breathing or anything. He knows I didn't choke him, because I still see him today.

If I was actually a threat, I wouldn't have been seeing him anymore. So both he and I know that I didn't choke him. He never stopped breathing. It wasn't bad at all.

He's a very tall guy. I kicked his leg and I just tried to back away. I wasn't choking him till he turned purple or blue – I was just trying to stop him. He came up to me from behind his desk, telling me I had to go to the hospital again. *You don't have a choice.* This would be the eighth time – and he's the doctor at this hospital he wants to send me to.

When people hear about it, they think, "Oh, you choked your psychiatrist," or, "Oh, he has anger issues." No. Most people in my situation would have done the exact same thing if they had also been hospitalized seven times, and were on their way to an involuntary – and unnecessarily forced – eighth visit.

*You don't have a choice.*

I just kind of put my hands around his neck, but I didn't fully grab. And I kicked his leg. My hands weren't on him for more than two seconds, probably not even one full second. It wasn't that big of a deal.

Of course, my dad was in the room, and he's a cop. So he got me down and sat on me until the cops got there. People say, "Oh wow, he's angry. He choked his psychiatrist. He has anger issues. I've never choked *my* psychiatrist." And I just want to ask, "Have you been hospitalized eight individual times? Were you hospitalized for more than 150 days?"

It wasn't anger. I didn't want to go to the hospital again. I was running away.

After that, I was hospitalized for over two weeks. And that's when they threatened a long-term stay for me at the state hospital. At the same time, my mom and sister emailed Dr. Phil. I heard the situation had to get to certain levels to be on the show. And I remember them saying that I was at the third level, then I was at the second level, then I was at the final level to decide if I'd be on the show. It was surreal, for sure. But again, a lot of my life is not surprising to me because I've become so used to unusual things. That's just the story of my life.

Then I get the news: I'll be on Dr. Phil. This is the second time in my life that I'd be on national television, the first being The Tonight Show.

I was still in the hospital a couple days before the Dr. Phil episode was taped. Funnily enough, on my discharge papers, the follow-up was listed as: "Dr. Phil."

---

# Chapter 12: *Dr. Phil*

A nurse always checks off with you for your follow-up. The eighth time I was discharged from the hospital, the nurse was a little surprised at what my documents said. "You're following up with Dr. Phil?" "Yes, that's correct," I said. Then I went home for a couple days after that.

I wasn't nervous about going on the Dr. Phil show. I was kind of relieved, actually. I was thinking to myself, "This is it. This is the answer. I have this big icon, this guy who has helped hundreds and hundreds of people, who's now going to help me." And at the time I respected Dr. Phil. You hear all these stories about him helping people. To some degree, however, I lost a lot of that respect after going on the show. But I hesitate to say I lost respect for Dr. Phil himself so much as I did for all the staff who work under him, and put the episodes together.

But I was so excited, even though I knew going into it that certain things would make me look bad. I was going to tell people my story. I was going to be transparent. And, yes, that might put me in a bit of a bad light.

What they didn't tell me was just how terrible they'd make me look.

The first problem was that they never really told me much of what was going to happen. I was told that, most likely, they'd be giving me a treatment. And that was the reason I was going to get to be on the show. And I was thinking to myself at the time how amazing it was, how phenomenal.

And, of course, Dr. Phil has a decent amount of money that he could put into treatment. As for me, I had never been one to reject treatment. There's never been one day when I wasn't open to something, anything, that might alleviate or fix this condition. "How am I gonna get rid of this?" is the question I'm always asking. So I was thrilled about the possibility of treatment on Dr. Phil.

When people think of those who go on the show, they often don't understand why anyone would want to embarrass themselves on national television like that. But the thing is, that's not what the people who go on the show are thinking. I didn't care about any of that. All I could think about was, "Wow, I'm actually going to be saved by Dr. Phil. He's going to change my life." Like the recovery stories you see of the people who were on the show and then came back to say how much better they were doing. There are tons of those people. The show helped so many. So why didn't they help me? Why doesn't the show contact me today?

I've probably tried a hundred times, myself and my parents, to reach out to the people who work for the show and the coordinator who is supposed to keep in touch with the patient. But he didn't; he stopped answering me and my parents and my other relatives who were trying to help out.

Nevertheless, during the moment I was so thrilled to go on the show. I thought I'd be sent to the best places too, like the office of a guy named Dr. Lawlis who apparently was Dr. Phil's mentor. But Dr. Lawlis didn't do anything for me. It was very sketchy when I went there, in fact.

So we get to the show, and it's me, my mother, my father, and my half-brother who is 10 years older than me. I found this last fact kind of comical. Out of all people, they chose him to talk about the family dynamic – he's a literal decade older than me, he has a different father, and he lives in New Jersey.

I've got three siblings my exact same age. You'd think they'd bring one of them onto the show. But my half-brother Blaise – I guess he knows some of what's going on in the house, but he doesn't really. He doesn't even live in the house. But he was the one to be willing to talk about me and say that I "terrorize" the family, which is his quotation that the show repeatedly used to describe me.

Now, Blaise told me before he went on the show that he was going to "say some harsh things, but we have to get on the show. We have to do this to help you." And the strange thing is that because of this, people thought we as a family were fighting a lot at the time I was on the show. But actually, we were getting along pretty well. We were pretty unified. The four of us slept in the same hotel room when we flew out to Los Angeles. We were getting along, hugging each other, saying "I love you" and all that. I even slept in the bed next to Blaise. And then he goes on the show and is practically forced to say all that stuff. He was doing anything in his power to help his brother whom he loves. There isn't a person who couldn't recognize the love as each of us were shedding tears, while being officially promised "treatment" from Dr. Phil within the final minutes of the episode.

The day before the taping, we did a bunch of interviews in a dark room with a spotlight on you. And you do some walking outside too, and a bunch of staged, stupid stuff like reenactments. For example, we did the reenactment of the choking (which wasn't really a choking) incident with the psychiatrist; but they obviously planned on cherry-picking the worst things from that and exaggerating everything, because that's what they did.

I talked about how he came across his desk. I didn't hop over his desk. I told the people in the interviews how the psychiatrist talked about 302'ing me, but they never mentioned that of course. I mentioned over and over what it's like and what it means to be depersonalized, which is the symptom of the condition I have, but they cut every time I used the word depersonalization. They just cut it out, because they didn't want it to seem like I had this disorder. Instead, they wanted to make it seem like I had this behavioral health problem, which was totally untrue.

The previews were absolutely terrible. If I ever want to get a job, or if anyone looks up my first and last name, they're gonna say something like, "Oh, Chase is the kid who choked his psychiatrist. He was on Dr. Phil." And that's not even correct. It's damaging my life and my future career, when and if I do get better. And that's depressing to think about.

And here's where I'd agree with all those people who ask, "Who would do that to themselves? Why would they be all right with going on the show?" I had *no idea* it was going to be like that though. The reason why I did that to myself is because I was certain I was going to get treatment. And that did not happen.

The show broke several promises. They told me they were going to send me to Onsite, which is this residential place out of Nashville, Tennessee. I wish I was just making this up, but I'm not. He told me the exact name of the exact place where I was going to go – and then never sent me there. Then they said they were going to do all these things, they're going to follow up, they're going to do this and that and blah blah blah. They never did.

It was even worse backstage with Dr. Phil. There's this guy named Anthony Haskins who works with him, and he kept saying that "We're not going to give up on you. Dr. Phil and I – we're not going to give up on your case. We're going to make sure that this is done." On a separate occasion behind the curtains, even, Dr. Phil personally told me that they would give me the help I need, that hopefully I could get rid of this disorder, and that he was going to get me better. And they never did those things.

That's extremely disappointing, because I see all these posts about drug addicts and people with serious behavioral problems, and they all get helped. But me – I actually have good intentions, and they never helped me.

The live show was the day after the interviews. The producer's name was Kimberly, I believe. And she told me, "Chase, use all the rage you have, and all the anger you have, out on that stage and you show your parents all the anger."

And I was like, "I'm not really angry at them. I just want to get through this." Because, of course, we were just there for the promise of treatment. We were also prepared to talk about our family issues on TV too – whatever. But the real reason we were there was for the treatment, and that only. I mean, that's the only reason I went there.

So this producer, she was telling me all this right before I was coming out on stage. She was trying to pump me up and get me going and fuming mad, which I wasn't at all. And she said to me, "Your parents told me that they actually didn't throw you out of the house." I talked to my parents after, and they said that that was a lie. I believe in my parents, and the whole weird scenario with the staff was utterly disgusting.

Months later, I saw an article about how the show's staff were putting alcohol and booze in the hotel rooms the show's guests were staying at. They were pushing them to make them look like fools so that the show would get better ratings. I'm not mad at Dr. Phil personally. I'm actually not mad at anyone. It's just very disappointing. I ruined my whole name, and my family's name too, for a treatment that was promised to me but never given – and for TV ratings that have absolutely no bearing on whether I, and the situation that my family is in, get better.

Even to this day, if I had looked like a fool but was at least relieved of my disorder, it would have been worth it, and then some. But the frustrating part is I never got better. And I still have to go through all this and pay out-of-pocket. The person who promised me didn't help me.

It's so comical if you look at it from an outside perspective with all the facts, and you don't watch the stupid previews or don't even watch the show. The whole thing was cherry-picked. I said a lot of other stuff that they just didn't put in.

At the time of the show, I was 19 and my half-brother Blaise was 29. And Dr. Phil kept going back to my half-brother to talk about the family dynamic and all that. Yet he didn't even live in the same state – come on, give me a break.

Then, they said that I stole my mother's car, and showed the reenactment of that. And he said, "He stole his mother's car and gave her the finger." And they used it to make this big dramatic thing. But it's so funny because what actually happened that day is totally different. I was just using the car to volunteer for someone I had promised to volunteer for that night. I left around 9 p.m., and I was back around 10 or 10:30 p.m. It was a very, very short event, yet they made this huge deal of it: "He stole his mother's car," almost implying that I went out for a full night or a few days to party or drink or just leave and never come back. But that was a way different tale than what actually happened.

People in the audience were gasping when Dr. Phil said I stole a car. They thought, "Wow, what a disrespectful kid, stealing a car." Well, I didn't really steal. I gave her back the car in a matter of hours and I went out volunteering. So when Dr. Phil said, "You stole your mother's car?" I could only think, no, not really. I didn't steal her car. I borrowed it for hours of volunteering that I promised to the guy I volunteer for. That's kind of funny.

But it's also sad because I'm a very positive person, and I always try to look at the bright side of things. I'm a lover. I don't hate anyone in this world. I don't hate anyone who ever existed. I'm not a hateful person – that's my whole philosophy, to never hate anyone. Because you never know their scenario, as so many people don't know mine.

## Chapter 13: *After Dr. Phil*

When I got home from Dr. Phil, I wasn't allowed to tell anyone about the show, and I couldn't post anything until the previews came out.

I signed something for it to be this way. That's another thing: I was in such a vulnerable position. I probably would get in trouble for talking about these things. I'm not allowed to say certain things. But, come on, I didn't know what I was signing – I couldn't read or concentrate. He took advantage of me. I wasn't in the right state of mind.

When I went home, I had a selfie picture with Dr. Phil. We also took a professional picture, and I was supposed to get that in the mail. But like so many other things, it didn't come.

I started dating someone during this time period too, right after the show. It feels really weird to date someone when you have depersonalization, because I was trying so hard to have a connection. During all my hospitalizations, three nurses even told me, "Maybe you should get a girlfriend." It was suggested quite a bit. So I said, yeah, okay, a girlfriend might actually work.

So I started dating this girl and I really liked her a lot. I had feelings for her, genuine feelings, but it was hard because I was having panic attacks on the road and she lived 25 minutes away.

I went out. So that was bad. But it wasn't really a relationship to me. There have been other times when I've tried talking to girls and all that stuff, but it just doesn't feel right. I know I'm not that stable and I know that, logistically, I should be independent, live on my own, be capable of holding a job, and so on. But right now, I can't even hold a part-time job. I can't even do a couple hours a week, if anything. And that's why I volunteer, because I can go on leave whenever I want. I can't deal with a lot of stress.

But dating was difficult. It kind of messed with my mind, too. I had two longer-term girlfriends before depersonalization. And those were very different from the relationships I had while having DP. Before, my relationships felt normal and I actually had strong chemistry with the girls. It's different now, though.

It's a little hard because they'll never understand what I've gone through. I especially can't even think about a wife right now. But if I'm going to get married someday, I don't have to marry someone with depersonalization. But I feel like the only person I could possibly marry would be someone who has suffered greatly from something.

I don't want my whole life to be about depersonalization. But I just probably need a woman who knows what suffering is like, to some extent.

Going back to what happened after Dr. Phil, his staff told me that the show was going to pay for 10 life coach sessions, and that was it. They did do that, and I personally love my life coach – but no matter how good a life coach is, it is never the same thing as a trained, highly-experienced professional with years of schooling and practice in the field working with people like me day in and day out. So all I've been coached for is very generic. And that's all they had to offer me, although they promised me way more and said they were going to send me to a residential place outside Nashville, which they never did.

Some part of me feels like if Dr. Phil saw me on the street after all this time of broken contact, his heart and soul would be good enough to care more about my case and continue on with it, because it's a very interesting and extraordinary case.

At any rate, that would be good to just bring the word "depersonalization" to a national level: what depersonalization is, how it affects someone, and how to spot it. It's much more common than people think. I know people in my area who have it – at least seven people within a 10-mile radius. That's insane to me.

One time I was at a graduation party and I was talking to a middle-aged woman. She asked me why I wasn't working. And I said, "Because I have this disorder called depersonalization-derealization disorder." And she said back to me, "Oh, I had that for a year, and then it went away."

That's another very interesting thing. A lot of times people will have it for a couple of years, and then it will go away. People pop in and out of the symptoms. And that, to me, is why the disorder is so fascinating in a sense. I've never heard of any disorder like this before. I know some people say it's a process, but there are so many stories where people are in it and then – *snap* – they're out of it. And that's why, in my opinion, the cause would be something physical, or something we really don't know much about.

In the past year or so, I've started dating again and started working, but I had to stop the latter real quick because I couldn't do it.

But then I went to two of these conferences with Jeff Abugel, who writes about depersonalization and derealization. He co-authored "Feeling Unreal" and was the sole author of "Stranger to My Self," both books about DPDR.

Sometimes I think about my own role in helping the DPDR community. For example, when the Dr. Phil thing was going viral on Facebook, I was getting messages every day from people all around the world, saying that they had the same exact thing and had gotten it from smoking a lot of marijuana or some other situation.

But I'm content to know I've talked people out of suicide, and I've been there for a lot of people who really needed someone. It's kind of funny; not only have I helped people with DP, but I've helped a lot of people with mental health in general. Sometimes you don't have to understand someone's specific disorder and specific symptoms to understand where they're coming from, and maybe even what they need. You can help and support people who are suffering mentally no matter if you've got the same thing as them. A lot of the people I've helped had crippling depression or panic disorders.

Since the show, I've been living at home. I work on music and I volunteer. Right now I'm seeing a Lyme specialist, and going to the Cleveland Clinic.

---

# Chapter 14: *Where I Stand*

Every single day I am trying to get better. I've kind of accepted that it's not necessarily a problem with my thoughts or my thinking. It's something physical, something we don't quite understand fully. So that's why I'm seeing a Lyme specialist right now, doing injection antibiotics and certain diets for a few months. But that hasn't really worked out so far.

The doctor that I'm supposed to see at the Cleveland Clinic is apparently good with unknown disorders, or understudied disorders, so we'll see how that goes.

I'd like to be a spokesman for depersonalization, and in a way I kind of already am. A lot of people in the depersonalization world know me. A lot of them message me as well.

I think my story is important to know because my life is so unique, and a lot of things are just unbelievable. So many crazy things have happened, but so much suffering as well – and I want to show what that is like, in the hope that I can help those people going through something similar. I think suffering can reveal some sort of beauty and some sort of positivity in life, and I want to spread that message.

I also sometimes think that, if you've been to that deepest depth, the deepest depths of suffering, you have a much better understanding of life – even better than some people who are 80 years old. You just gain a lot of wisdom from suffering like this, especially when you're suffering from something that people don't know well.

You're a warrior in disguise. You're suffering and people can't see it all. You're suffering and it's from a disorder that's not really recognized. But it should be. And there are so many people out there with it. The extent is unbelievable.

This will be a movement, and not just your cliché mental health movement. I want this to be as real as it can get. I want to show the realness of mental health in all its forms and depths. I'm aware of how people use it, but I really want to reveal what it actually is and try to express it as best as I can in words.

I hope I have at least partly succeeded with that here.

---

# *Epilogue*

Mental health is all we have. If we don't have decent mental health, then nothing in our life matters. Before all this happened to me, I was ignorant about mental illness as a whole.

But now, I have learned just to love everyone – literally anyone in this beautiful, disastrous world. It's difficult to scold someone who innocently doesn't understand, but you just have to go one step further as a sufferer of any sort and realize they will never get it, let alone understand. Your pain is unfathomable. If someone has never been in the situation you are or have been in, you most likely would speak and act identically toward your family and friends. If you are suffering, grasp onto any moments of pleasure you get, even if it's for a second. Don't pressure yourself. You do whatever you need to do at the time. You come first. It's your life. You are the most important person in the world.

Everyone is affected by mental illness, whether you have it yourself or if you know someone who does. If you aren't the person suffering and your loved one is, you just have to do one thing. Be open. Just focus on that single objective: being open. You do not have to fix them. You do not have to understand. You even do not have to attempt to comprehend it. Just be open. Be aware of their pain and listen. Really try to listen to what they are saying or trying to say, no matter how ridiculous or unbelievable it may sound. Just absorb and be open. No need to play doctor. Do not attempt to relate when you simply cannot.

The most help I have ever gotten from others was from people who were open-minded, good listeners. The "fixers" were the least helpful – if anything, they were damaging. The thing about fixers is that they always have good intent; to a sufferer, however, they come across as a "know-it-all." The reality is they don't know it all. Some of those people have the biggest hearts and want what they think is the absolute best for the sufferer. But they do not know what is best for the sufferer. Not even the professionals who, with various degrees, globally recognized experience in the field, and decades of exposure to multitudes of mental disorders – not even they know what's best for the sufferer. This is why we need to put the spotlight on this specific disorder. And mental health as a whole.

People need to know there is a difference between dissociation, anxiety, depression, and psychosis. There is such a negative connotation with all of these terms, including "mental illness" as well. If you are mentally ill, that does not mean you are crazy. People with an anxiety disorder are mentally ill. People with depression are mentally ill. They aren't considered crazy. Dissociation (which DDD falls under) shouldn't be considered crazy. Just because we use metaphors to attempt to describe our sensation does not mean we are delusional. We are not. Is it possible for those terms to overlap? Of course. We are not crazy.

I used to misuse the words anxiety, depression, and OCD. Most people do. Anxiety is not nervousness.

Depression isn't sadness. OCD doesn't mean organized. It gets tiring to hear people misuse these terms. I think it is extremely important to not misuse these because it diminishes from the actual sufferers. I am not being judgmental one bit toward anyone by expressing this, because I plead guilty for this even to this day. It has become second nature to me. If you say "I have anxiety for this test tomorrow," are you actually experiencing anxiety or are you just really nervous? Are you having a legitimate panic attack? Or are you just having a mental breakdown? When you listen to a sad song or hear something heartbreaking, are you depressed or are you just sad?

If you are suffering from clinical depression, you would be isolating yourself, developing insomnia, and losing all pleasure from everyday activities. We all know when it snows people joke around about having seasonal depression. (This is an actual thing, although commonly misused.) Another common example: if you see papers that are not in line and you fix them and say, "Sorry my OCD is kicking in" – most likely when you say that you do not have OCD, otherwise you would be suffering, probably on medications for it, and seeing a therapist.

In no way am I commanding you to change how you speak or anything. The only thing I ask from you is to be open to any mentally ill sufferer whom you care for, cherish, or love. It is beneficial to be aware of how you are handling someone else and their specific situation. Being open is key. Awareness leads to being open, which then leads to acceptance. Simple – being aware helps to become open. Reading this now is completing the first step, awareness.

My pot story is not as uncommon as you may think. In the movie "Numb" from 2007, the main character develops depersonalization disorder immediately after smoking marijuana. The entire movie revolves around DPDR and the disorder; its main character is world-renowned actor Matthew Perry, most famous for his role as Chandler in the sitcom "Friends." It also features Mary Steenburgen and more. The movie is not the best description of DDD because, keep in mind, a movie needs to have other entertainment factors. It is just a wonderful exposure of depersonalization. Marijuana is one of the most popular triggers (not causes) to DDD, in addition to PTSD, Lyme disease, stress, and other disorders.

DDD is debilitating and comes with pure suffering, plain and simple. And this is coming from a guy who didn't believe in mental illness prior to getting it. Not only did I not believe its legitimacy, but I diminished the suffering of those who really had it, and thought they were ungrateful and idiotic. So I had to learn the hard way and receive probably the all-time highest possible level of human pain. Daily I assume people just see the hell I live in sticking out like a sore thumb, but they cannot at all. That's one of the worst parts of suffering from a chronic, unknown condition; but I am so grateful none of my loved ones have to suffer from this. If this happened to them and not me, how would I be acting? Exactly like them.

Thousands of people are being misdiagnosed and thrown into long-term mental health care units. Getting drugged up and institutionalized. Why does a disorder only have to be schizophrenia or psychosis if it isn't anxiety or depression? There is another disorder: depersonalization derealization disorder. A crippling, understudied dissociative disorder. Dissociation is its own branch of mental illness. Dissociation is different than anxiety and depression.

We will get this disorder out there and make depersonalization and derealization household terms. We will continue putting the spotlight on mental health as it's been a hot topic these days with all tragedies occurring daily across the nation. We are suffering with our mental health all around the globe. Ideally, we will one day eliminate these horrendous conditions. They are inhumane. No one chooses them. No one deserves it. No one.

I never knew it was possible to suffer this much and to this extent. It is unbelievable. My concept of time is lost. Panic attacks left and right. Depression. Dissociation. Anxiety. This is a living hell. In a deranged way, it is so beautiful as the pain decimates you. People commonly mistake the word "beauty" with the word "comfort." Sometimes the most incredibly beautiful things are by far the most uncomfortable, though they always produce beauty.

I love everyone in this world. I am beyond grateful for so many people who have actually been there for me. It means a lot.

This sure has aged me – my soul at least. I feel like I have lived on this planet for hundreds of years, but I am only 20. I just yearn for relief. Being content and being happy would be total luxuries.

Beauty is beauty. Beauty is neither good nor bad; it's just – beauty.

---

55534458R00046